Stratocaster Setup

Including how to tune a guitar, how to tune a guitar by ear, how to change guitar strings and how to set guitar intonation and guitar action on all guitars

Jan Nasser

First Printing, 2012

ISBN-13: 978-1478349525

ISBN-10: 1478349522

Printed in the United States of America

Dedication

For Alan who keeps helping me strive for more

Stratocaster Setup

Including how to tune a guitar, how
to tune a guitar by ear, how to
change guitar strings and how to set
guitar intonation and guitar action
on all guitars

Table of Contents

Introduction

In the main the Fender Stratocaster guitar is just the same as any other electric guitar and setting it up involves the same kinds of skills. The hardware maybe slightly different but all the parts are recognizable as standard guitar parts such as the bridge, nut and machine heads. As a result this book covers all the setup details of guitars in general with the important extra bits that you need in order to get your Stratocaster really humming.

When using this book you should note that there is a particular order to the things that you set up. If you change the order you may find that you will have to go back and redo some of the tasks because you have changed things once again. The final thing that you should do is set up the guitar intonation. This is because changing the gauge of strings, adjusting the action and setting the truss rod could all change the intonation settings. If you are simply changing your strings for the same gauge as you were previously using there shouldn't be a need to do any further adjustments as the existing settings should be just right.

The book starts with sections on tuning and solving tuning problems because you need a guitar that stays in tune in order to do further set up tasks on it. The book assumes that you will have an electronic guitar tuner. This will allow you to make precise settings which will improve the overall performance and sound of the guitar. If you have a good sense of pitch then you can, of course, use your ears. Without an electronic tuner you can tackle all of the set up tasks apart from the setting of intonation which requires more accurate settings.

You need to really know what you want to achieve before you start changing things on your guitar. If you are a complete beginner, at playing the guitar, it probably isn't a good idea for you to start changing the settings on your instrument. You should therefore get a professional or more experienced guitarist to look at any problems that you have, until you know exactly what you want.

You don't have to read the book right of the way through. You can simply dip in and out and pick out the part that you want to focus on. However, please remember as stated before that changes that you make may have knock on effects on other guitar settings.

Other tools you will require include some decent wire cutters, set of Phillips screwdrivers, Capo, feeler gauges and hex spanners to adjust the bridge and truss rod.

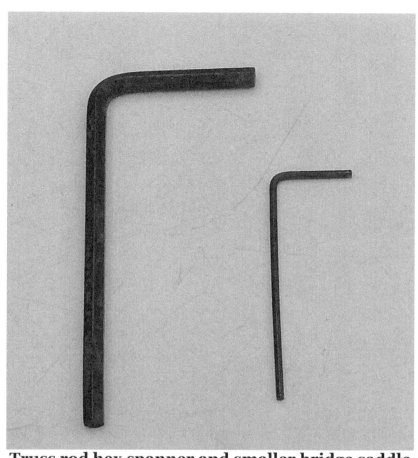

Truss rod hex spanner and smaller bridge saddle spanner

Tuning your guitar

In order to set up your guitar it is essential that you manage to get it in tune in the first place. You should tune to the standard tuning open string notes of E, A, D, G, B, E or otherwise the tuning that you intend to use on the guitar. When setting up make sure that these are at standard concert pitch. If you tune the guitar to itself you will find that it will be off pitch unless you use a standard reference note to start with. You can get a reference note from such things as guitar pitch pipes, tuning fork or keyboards. The easiest way to tune your guitar is to use an electronic tuner. These are relatively cheap, these days, and even the simplest one will do a good job.

The importance of having your guitar at standard pitch is that the tension on the strings will be correct. This in turn will mean that the tension on the neck will be correct too. When you tune your guitar with new strings on, make sure that the strings have been stretched slightly by pulling them away from the fret board a few times until they remain in tune. Always tune your string from a lower note than you want to tune to. This will mean that you are always tightening the string as it moves towards the correct note. If you tune from above the note you can end up leaving slack on the windings which will be released later and cause your guitar to go out of tune.

How to set up a guitar that stays in tune

All guitars can suffer from tuning problems and solving them can involve a lot of checking, adjusting, testing and then checking once again. As with all trouble shooting and repairing you need to focus on changing one thing at a time and then checking to see if the tuning problem has been resolved. With mechanical systems you have to consider all of the places where problems might occur. These areas include:

Strings
Machine heads
String trees
Nut
Frets
Bridge
Tremolo system
Tail piece

All of these different parts have to be working correctly in order for your guitar to remain in tune. The strings interact with these parts and as a result they may snag on rough or poorly angled pieces as they are tuned up resulting in tension building up in windings and on surfaces that the string passes over. This tension may be suddenly released and this will result in the string going out of tune.

You may notice a clinking sound as you tune up the strings. This is a sure indication that the string is snagging on something. You should listen and try to identify where it is happening. Once you have done this you can examine the suspect guitar part more closely to try and identify the problem. Without any indications like this it is a case of inspecting each part along the path of the string to see if there are rough surfaces, worn or loose moving parts or even missing screws or broken pieces. The older an instrument is the more likely that the parts are going to suffer from mechanical failure. You should keep this in mind when you check them out.

In this section it is suggested that you can use powdered graphite as a lubricating agent. This is good stuff because it won't damage surfaces and finishes in the way that oil based lubricants can. The easiest way to obtain powdered graphite is from pencil lead. Simply rub the pencil lead over a rough surface such as a piece of fine sand paper or emery board and then collect the graphite to coat the surfaces that you want to lubricate.

Here are some of the problems that you might encounter once you start examining the surfaces that the strings have to pass over.

Strings

The strings themselves are rarely the problem unless they are very old and worn. However, if you change the gauge of your strings and do no further adjustments to the guitar you may find that the guitar appears to go out of tune as you play it. However, if you check the tuning of the open string it will still be in tune. This is a problem of guitar intonation and you should therefore go to the section on adjusting intonation for a fix.

Sometimes cheap strings may be poorly manufactured and this can lead to tuning problems. The windings at the string loop end may start to unwind and this will mean that the string slowly gets slacker. If you suspect that this is the case then you should replace the suspect string or replace the whole set if you think they aren't up to the job.

The main issue with strings as far as tuning is concerned revolves around how well they are put on the guitar in the first place. Older Fender Stratocaster have what are called vintage machine heads and these have a unique design with a slot in the top to feed the string through rather than the more usual hole in the side of the tuning peg on most other guitars.

Slot headed machine heads can give problems to people trying to fit strings. You either love them or hate them. The most common problem concerns the B and E strings because they can pop out of the slot as you are fitting them and this means that you have to try and put them back on. This is more difficult because the string will now have some windings in it rather than being straight. If you have to do this a number of times you may find that the string will break. I personally really like the slot heads because with good technique for fitting them you can reduce the problems of them springing out of the slot. Once on, the strings fitted to a slot head machine head tend to stay in tune more readily than the side hole version. This is because the slot and windings fix the string in position on the spindle of the machine head and prevent slipping while playing. I like them so much that I changed the ordinary machines heads on my 1982 Stratocaster for the slot heads.

17

One of the keys to success with both types is to keep pressure on the string all of the time, by pulling it towards the body end, as you wind the string on. When fitting strings you can either fit them one at a time and remove each old string just before fitting the new one or you can take all of the strings off at the start and then fit them. The advantage of fitting and removing them one at a time is that you only have to deal with tuning one string at a time. If you take them all off it can take a while for the springs in the tremolo system to reach the correct tension and this can mean a lot of tuning and retuning of the guitar to start off with. The advantage of removing all of the strings at the start is that you can clean up the fret board and make sure that it is nice to play.

Fitting strings to vintage slot head machine heads:

You will need some wire cutters, Phillips head screwdriver and an electronic tuner. You will also find that a string winder is also helpful. The first thing to do is to remove the plastic plate on the back of the guitar covering the bottom of the tremolo system and the tail piece block. This will allow you to remove the strings from the body more easily. Start with the bass E string. Slacken of the string and pull it off the tuning peg. This should be easy to do with the slot head as once the string is slackened it will simply pull out and straight off. At this point you can either try to straighten out the windings a little so that they will pull back through the bridge/tremolo holes or cut off the end of the string so that the windings are removed. I prefer the cutting method because there are no windings to get caught in the bridge and tremolo system.

Once the string is cut you should take care with the cut ends because they tend to be a lot sharper than the ordinary ends of the string. You should therefore make sure that you don't cut yourself when taking the string off the guitar. Push the string back through the body and remove it from the tail piece block.

Remove the new string from the pack and unwind it so that it is straight. Push the string up through the tail piece block and then through the hole in the body and the hole in the tremolo/bridge plate. Pull the string through so that it sits solidly in the tail piece recess. You can check this by looking at the back of the guitar.

Turn the machine head so that the slot is following the same line as the neck and then lay the string in the slot and pull from the other side so that it is hand tight. Take the wire cutter and cut the string so that it goes about 2 to 3 inches after the slot of the machine head. This is about the width of 3 fingers. Once the string has been cut remove it from the slot and then poke the cut end down into the machine head slot so that it fits into the hole at the bottom. Once it is in the hole, bend the string into the slot and hold it with your right hand in place by both pushing the string down towards the fret board and making it go through the correct slot in the nut.

Next put some tension on the string by pulling it down towards the bridge end of the body. Wind the machine head so that the string starts to tighten. Keep the string low towards the head stock so that the windings form above where the string meets the machine head spindle. Continue winding and applying tension to the string letting it slip through your fingers as the windings form. Once the string is tight enough you can release the tension from it and the windings should stay in place on the machine head. The concave shape of the tuning peg tends to make the windings on it tighten up against each other and this in turn helps to reduce tuning problems as the string is less likely to slip and unreleased tension in the windings is eliminated. Continue to tighten up the string until you get it to concert pitch as shown by your electronic tuner.

It is important to try and remove any slack in the string that has been caused by winding it onto the tuning peg. To do this, pull the string away from the body stretching it. This will tend to make the windings lie more evenly and tighten them up against the tuning peg. You can then repeat this procedure with the A, D and G strings tuning them up as you go

Vintage slot head machine heads

As mentioned before most people have more trouble with the B and E strings because they are so much thinner. However the technique is really just the same. But you need to make sure that you apply enough tension to the string both towards the head stock and towards the body of the guitar. If you do have problems you can try bending the string with your finger nail before you push it into the hole. You then cut the string after the bend allowing about ½ inch of the string end to go into the hole. Push the end of the string into the hole and the bent part through the slot. You can then manually wind the string round half way to the other side of the slot and then pull it back through the slot. Make sure that you are winding the string on in the correct direction though. Try to manually wind the string round the tuning peg normally for a couple of turns before applying tension to the string as already described above. By pulling the string back through the slot after half a turn at the start you are essentially locking the string onto the machine head. This has the effect of both stopping it springing off the tuning peg and helping to stop any string slippage which might cause tuning problems.

Fitting strings to modern side hole machine heads:

The technique for doing this follows pretty much the same idea as used in the case of the vintage machine heads. As a result, old strings are usually removed one at a time. Simply slacken the string at the machine head and then unwind and straighten or cut the old string. Remove the old string from the body and replace it with the new one as described above for vintage machine heads.

The difference occurs in how you attach the string to the machine head itself. In order to do this, firstly turn the hole in the tuning peg so that it is in line with the run of the neck. Poke the string through the hole and pull it hand tight. Next pull the string back through the hole in the tuning peg about 3 inches. Bend the string end downwards and round the machine head and under the string as it comes from the body towards the machine head. Bend the end of the string back over the string until the end is pointing upwards.

Pass The string under and then point it up

At this point make sure that you have some tension with your one hand pulling the string back towards the body. This should trap the string in position. Turn the machine head so that it lays windings over the upward pointing end of the string. You may need to keep adjusting the end of the string so that it still points upwards. Once the string begins to tighten you can stop pulling back on it. The idea behind this method is that the successive layers of string windings trap the end of the string up against the tuning peg. The more that you stretch the string the tighter the windings on the machine headbecome. The net result is that the harder you work the strings the less likely the windings are to slip and therefore tuning remains constant.

Once you have the string to concert pitch stretch it a few times and retune until it remains in tune. You can now use the wire cutters to cut the upward pointing string end level with the top of the tuning peg. Stretch the strings, as detailed for the vintage machine heads, retuning each time until it becomes stable. Play the guitar for a few minutes and check the tuning and retune if necessary.

Machine heads

The machine heads are probably one of the weakest points in the string path as far as mechanical problems are concerned. They get a lot of use so if your Strat is old it might be time to renew them. If you suspect that a particular machine head is causing tuning problems then the first stage is to check that it is securely attached to the headstock. There should be screws in the case of the machine head which secure it to the back of the headstock. Check to see that they are all present and that they are tightened up. I have sometimes come across instruments where the machine head is lifting away from the headstock due to poorly fitted screws. This can cause the machine head to rock about and in turn lead to tuning problems.

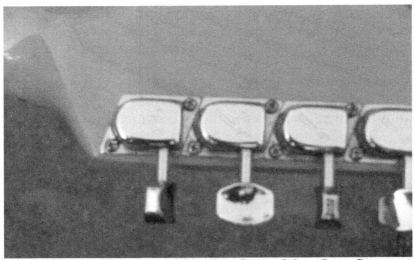

Screw fixings on back of machine heads

Each machine head has a central spindle around which the string windings form. Remove the string from the suspect machine head and try to rock the spindle from side to side. The spindle should be solidly fixed to the metal mounting of the machine head. If this is not the case and it moves a lot then this could also cause tuning problems. Most machine heads are sealed units these days so the only the thing that you can do is to replace them if they are slipping. In other designs the back plate comes off with the retaining screws. In this case remove the machine head back casing and look at where the spindle is fixed to the back plate. There should be a large screw located there. Tighten the screw up so that the spindle is once again securely fitted to the back plate.

The machine heads can be implicated in tuning problems purely because the strings haven't been put on the guitar in a good way. If you suspect that this might be one of the problems you should look at the section about stringing your guitar.

String Trees

String trees are something particular to Fender style guitars. This is due to the way that the necks are produced. Most other guitars have quite a steep angle where the headstock attaches to the neck. This means that the strings are kept close to the headstock and that they follow a natural path to the machine head which tends to keep them in place. If you next look at a Fender neck you will see that there really isn't any angle at all between the neck and the headstock. The string trees are therefore an addition to the headstock in order to try and keep the strings in position so that they don't easily float out of the slots in the nut. The string trees therefore give yet another place for unreleased tension to develop. There isn't much that you can do to adjust them other than checking that they are securely positioned in place and that the strings actually go underneath them. The finish on these can deteriorate over time and in damp atmospheres so you need to inspect the underside of the trees to make sure that they are smooth and without areas of corrosion which might snag the strings. Clean these up so that the strings rest against a nice smooth surface. You can also lubricate these with some graphite powder.

Check string trees for corrosion and lubricate with graphite

Later roller style string trees

Nut

The nut can present a tight area for the strings to pass through which certainly can catch and snag the strings as they pass through the narrow grooves. Nuts on guitars straight from the factory shouldn't present any problems. On older guitars they are likely to have suffered wear and even damage. Previous owners of guitars may also have tried to reshape the grooves and ended up bodging the whole thing. One guitar that I bought had such problems. The previous owner had resorted to pushing match sticks into the grooves to increase the height of the strings at the head stock end of the guitar, You need to check carefully that nothing like this has happened to your Strat. In such a case the only thing to do is to get the nut replaced. Replacing a nut isn't something that you can easily do at home as you have to have specialized expensive files to cut the slots in it. If the nut slots are too narrow or too wide then once again you may need to replace it. You can get a graphite nut put on which will lubricate the strings as they pass through the grooves and hence prevent snagging and tension build up.

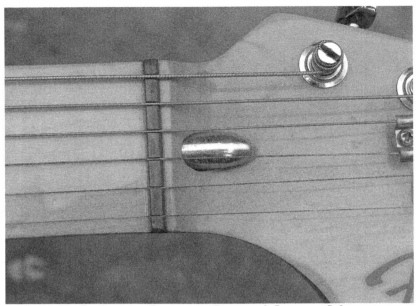

Lubricate the nut slots with graphite

Again the key to servicing the nut is to ensure that the surfaces of the grooves are nice and smooth. To start off with you can take the correct string for each groove size and run it through the groove a few times. The surfaces of the string will wear away and rough surfaces. This really works more for the wound strings rather than the thinner solid strings. Don't do this too much because it will steadily make the groove larger.

The next thing to do is to lubricate the grooves in the nut so that the strings will be able to move more freely when the machine heads are turned to tune the instrument. Don't use oils for this as the can damage the finish of the guitar especially if you have a lacquered fret board. The best thing to use once again is powdered graphite. Tip this into the grooves and the run the string through a few times to coat the inner surfaces of the groove.

Check for damage to the nut especially above and below the E strings. If the edge of the nut is damaged the string may wander about too much causing tuning problems. Once again in this situation you would need to replace the nut.

Frets

The frets themselves should be in the right position unless you have a really cheap guitar that wasn't made very well.

However, if your guitar has a high action or you have recently adjusted the action you may find that it appears to be out of tune when you fret strings even though the open strings are actually in tune. This is again a problem of intonation and you should therefore check and adjust it as described in the later chapter.

Sometimes frets are set quite high. This is great for increasing the wear that they can withstand but presents a problem from a playing point of view which may cause you to think the guitar is not in tune. The reason for this is that if you press down really hard on the fret the string is caused to stretch as you press it into the gap between the frets. There are 2 cures for this situation. The first is to learn to play more gently and not press the strings down too hard. The second would involve having the frets stoned down so that they have a lower relief above the fret board. The cheapest option is to play more gently. Some guitarists use this as an effect in their playing. They may even cut down further into the fret board giving what is called a scalloped neck so that they can stretch the strings even further. You need to make up your mind what is best for you and your playing.

Bridge

The bridge has a number of places that can cause problems as far as tuning is concerned. In the case of a Stratocaster guitar the strings pass over individual bridge saddles which can be adjusted to produce the best string height and intonation for the guitar. See the sections on intonation and action for details on how to adjust your bridge correctly.

Stratocaster bridge showing areas where corrosion may occur

The bridge saddles themselves can become worn and corroded and once again they can cause the string to snag and unreleased tension to build up in the string. If the saddle is heavily worn then you should replace it with a new one. Corrosion is a particular problem for the bridge hardware. This is because constant use of the right hand during playing to dampen the strings can release sweat onto the strings and hardware. It is this sweat that corrodes away the surface of the bridge saddles. As well as this skin cells and sweat can accumulate in any crevices and around the small hex bolts or screws used to adjust the bridge saddles.

Every now and then you should make sure that the bridge screws are not corroded into the holes by turning them slightly. If there is any doubt you should remove the screws from the saddle and clean them before replacing and lubricating with a little machine oil. If you don't do this, you will find that when you come to have to use the set up screws they won't turn. This could mean that you will have to replace the particular bridge saddle completely. If there is any corrosion you should use a hard bristle brush to clean it up and return to a nice smooth surface. Some metal polish might also help. Once this is done lubricate the surface of the saddle with a little graphite powder or light machine oil. Machine oil is often better here because it can stop sweat getting into strings at this point and reduce corrosion and metal fatigue which can cause strings to break. Check that the string passes over the centre of the saddle and has an unimpeded path down to the hole in the base plate that allows the string to pass through the body to the tail piece block. Check that the holes in the base plate aren't corroded and if they are clean them up with a brush and lubricate once again with graphite. Check that the holes in the base plate line up with the holes in the body and if they don't make sure that the bridge and tremolo unit are attached to the body securely. You can use a round needle file to widen the holes in the wooden body if the string appears to catch on it.

Tremolo system

The tremolo system can give rise to a lot of tuning issues especially if you use it a lot and use it with extreme movements where the strings go very loose. It is important to set up you tremolo unit correctly and so you should look at the section about this later on in the book. Again it is important that the strings once loosened are allowed to return easily to their natural position on all of the hardware items so far described. Use the tremolo slowly and see how the strings react and the surfaces that they have to move over. Once you have checked this make sure that these surfaces are corrosion free and well lubricated.

Tail piece

The tail piece on a Stratocaster is simply a large metal block with holes in it through which the strings pass. The metal ring in the end of the string is able to pass up into the block until it gets to a restriction where only the string itself can pass. You should check that the string is able to easily slide up to the stop point without getting snagged on the way. If this doesn't happen, use a needle file to wear away any obstructions that there might be. The obstructions may snag the string but then not hold it securely once string bending and tremolo playing are undertaken.

Check strings fit easily in tail piece to end stops

Setting the action

The action of the guitar is all about how close the strings are to the frets. Guitarists talk about guitars having a high or low action. This once again refers to the distance between the strings and the frets. High action means that the strings are far away from the frets. Guitarists also talk about instruments having a fast action. This relates to how fast and easily you can move about the fret board while you are playing. The higher that the action is set the further and harder that you have to press the strings in order to fret them. On the other hand a low action means that you only have to press the strings a short way for them to come into contact with the frets. This means that it is also easier to do because you don't have to stretch the strings much to reach the frets and this means less force is needed. Guitars with a low action are therefore easier to play. This can make life easier for people who are just starting to play. A low action also means that without having to put a lot of effort into pressing the strings down you can move across the fret board more quickly.

Low action settings on a guitar therefore result in easy and fast playing. However, the overall effect on the guitar isn't quite as simple as this. When you gain in one respect you can lose in other respects as far as the playing of the guitar is concerned. Bringing the strings nearer to the frets can mean that the strings will rattle on the higher frets on the fret board as you play. This will introduce extra rattling noises into the sound of the guitar. This can make the sound produced undesirable. This problem can be dramatically increased if the frets themselves aren't level along the length of the fret board. You will find that the rattling is therefore worse on some areas of the neck. If certain frets are higher than others you may find that the sound is completely choked off. This usually only happens in a few places on the neck. As a result the more even that the frets are in height across the fret board the lower that you can set the action of your guitar.

In addition to this, general wear through playing can put grooves into the frets especially in those areas of the fret board that you use a lot. This once again makes the fret board uneven and increases rattle and string choking. Setting action is therefore a compromise between how low you want the strings to be and how much noise and string choking that you can put up with. Usually guitarists can put up with some rattle but find that string choking is something that is unacceptable.

Electric guitars seem to be less susceptible to rattle once the signal is amplified so you should always test your Strat through an amplifier rather than just relying on the sound it produces when it is unplugged.

Although guitarists dream of a low action guitar they recognize the deterioration in sound that results from it. In the end the action setting of your guitar depends on personal preference. In my case I gladly give up having a very low action so that the strings sound cleaner and brighter when played. As you become more experienced at playing, very low actions become less important. It is all a mater of personal choice. In order to make sure that you can set up the action of your guitar well you should first make sure that the frets are even and not worn and you should also ensure that the bend of the neck is also set up correctly. You should see the section on truss rods to set the bend in the neck. If your frets are very uneven you would need to take your instrument to a luthier in order to have them stoned down so that they are even and without groove wear.

The action on a guitar is achieved by adjusting the height of the bridge saddles. Each string has its own individual saddle on a Stratocaster so you can concentrate on one string at a time. Each saddle has 2 hex screws which pass through it allowing it to rest on the bridge plate. You need to find the correct size of hex spanner for your particular saddle screws. There is usually one provided with the guitar to do this job when it is bought new. If you haven't got this, then you will need to buy one from a tool shop or DIY store. It is important that you use the right size spanner because it is easy to damage these small screws. Certainly don't try to bodge a screw driver down the head of one of these screws because that will certainly damage it.

Using hex spanner to adjust action on the G string

Start with the bass E string and work across to the high E string. Play the string along its length on all the frets. Listen out for problem areas of the fret board where rattles are high or string choking occurs. If you get string choking then you will need to tighten the bridge screws so that the bridge saddle is lifted. Tighten the screws a little at a time and then check the effect on the playability of the string. Do this until the choking stops. Make sure you adjust the screws on each side of the saddle by the same amount so that the saddle remains level. If you have just a few rattles or none at all you may decide that you can reduce the action of the string. Unscrew the hex screws a little at time and each time check to if rattling has increased. Once you have achieved a balance between the action that you would like and the amount of string buzz and rattling you should move onto the next string. Continue to do this until you have set the action of all of the strings.

Using hex spanner to adjust action on the D string

If you look at the bridge from the string side you should see that the saddles make a curved profile which should be similar to the curve of the fret board. If you haven't got an even curve you should investigate the strings that appear to be out of the curve and check that you have set them up the same as the others. The curve of the saddles should make it comfortable for your right hand to rest on it during playing and string dampening. If it isn't then you can even out the curve by adjusting the screw on one side of each saddle until a smooth curve is achieved. Make sure that you check the string concerned each time for extra rattle and buzz. You should then play your guitar for a while to make sure that you have the action that you want without excessive string rattle and buzz. If this is not the case you should go back and adjust the saddles once again until you are happy with the result.

Adjusting Fender neck tilt

A lot of Fender Stratocaster guitars have a neck tilt adjustment. This is useful if you run out of adjustment for setting the action of the guitar using the bridge screws. By adjusting the neck tilt you can bring the strings closer to the frets and therefore you need less bridge adjustment to set the action. The neck tilt adjuster is situated on the neck back plate. Stratocasters have a bolt on neck and there are either 3 or 4 screws in the back plate to bolt the neck to the body. If there is a tilt adjuster it will be accessed via a hole in the plate at the body end.

You need a 1/8 inch hex spanner to do the adjustment. This is usually the same adjuster as that used for the truss rod. You should have been given one of these with the tools that came with the guitar. The first stage in tilt adjustment is to slightly loosen the screws that bolt the neck to the body. This will give some room for the tilt to be adjusted. Relax the screws about half a turn. Then loosen the screws nearest the centre of the body another 1½ turns. Insert the hex spanner into the tilt adjuster and screw it in about half a turn. Retighten the neck bolts and then check to see the effect. You should tighten the bolts furthest from the adjuster first and then those nearest to it. Be careful when doing this as you don't want to over tighten them as this can strip the threads off the thread inserts in the neck. Turn the adjuster once more with the wrench until you feel some resistance. This will stop it rattling about and causing unwanted vibrations. The strings should now be closer to the fret board and this will give more room for action adjustment using the bridge saddle hex screws.

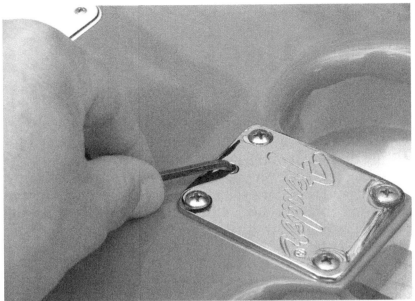

Neck tilt adjustment on a 4 bolt neck

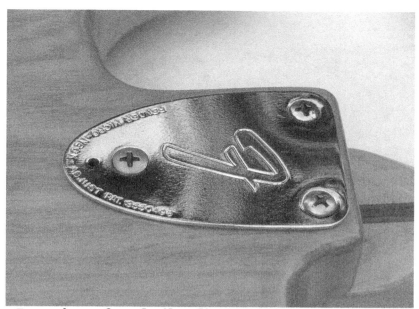

Location of neck tilt adjuster in 70's 3 bolt neck

The necks on Stratocaster guitars do tend to be rather straight out when compared to other style guitars and as a result using the neck tilt screw can make the angle of the neck a little more pleasing if that is what you like. However, you need to make sure that the effect on the bridge end isn't too drastic. You can only adjust the angle of the neck such that the bridge adjustment can accommodate the changes that you make on it.

Stratocaster pickup heights

The basic or vintage Stratocaster pickups are basically the same as on other electric guitars and work in the same way. Each pickup consists of a single long coil of insulated copper wire wound round 6 permanent cylindrical magnets. The magnets are the things that we refer to as the string pole pieces. The coil and magnets are fitted to a solid base with a plastic cover over them with holes that allow the pole pieces to project out under the strings. There is one magnetic pole piece for each string. Unlike other electric guitar pickups the Fender ones have the pole piece heights set at the factory and you can't adjust them individually.

When a string vibrates above the pickup the movement of the string disturbs the magnetic field created by the pickup. This disturbance causes an electrical voltage to be created in the coil of the pickup. This is the electrical signal which then travels down the wires from the pickup, through the guitar volume and tone controls and then through the guitar lead to the amplifier.

The quality and size of the electric signal produced depends upon a number of things. Heavier gauge strings mean more disturbance of the magnetic field and therefore a more powerful signal is produced by the pickup. As a result heavier strings tend to sound louder than lighter strings. The nearer that the string is to the magnetic field the greater the magnetic disturbance and the louder the signal produced by the pickup. On this basis it would seem that we should get the pickups as close to the strings as possible in order to get the best possible signal. This is true to a large extent, but things tend to go wrong when the strings are very close to the pickups. The main thing that happens is that the strings are attracted to the permanent magnet pole pieces of the pickup. This attraction causes them to stop vibrating in the normal way that a string should do. The net result is that rather than the signal getting louder the attraction causes the string to stop vibrating and the signal to get quieter. In extreme circumstances, when the string is so close to a pickup pole piece, it can hit it and even stick to it. All of this leads to a poor quality signal to be produced. As with everything there is a compromise that has to be set up. We need the pickup close enough to produce a large signal but not too close that its smooth vibration is disturbed.

Another thing to consider when setting pickups up is the balance of the sound produced. The thicker strings have more metal in them and therefore produce a bigger signal than the thinner ones. As a result in order to get the strings to produce a nice balanced sound we need to set the pickups further away from the thicker strings and closer to the thinner strings. In addition to this the profile of the fret board means that the strings also follow a curved profile when the action of the guitar is set up correctly. The factory setting of the pole piece heights is therefore designed to take this into consideration and compensate for it.

The only adjustment that you can make with the classic single coil pickups on a Stratocaster involves the use of the screws at the top and bottom of the pickup which attach it to the scratch plate. These screws fit directly through the scratch plate and into the threaded base plate of the pickup. There is a spring between the scratch plate and the base of the pickup. This means that turning the screw will adjust the height of the pickup above the scratch plate but won't allow it to wobble about once the adjustment is complete. When it comes to pickup adjustment you should once again make sure that you start with fresh new strings. Old worn strings tend to produce less sound and an unbalanced sound so you are best to use the new ones.

Despite the limitations in the adjustments that you make to the pickups on a Stratocaster the actual settings of them is very important if you want to achieve the classic sound of this guitar. This is one reason that most people don't even look at them once they have the guitar. Although this idea works it is also the case that, if you have adjusted such things as action and string gauge, you may be able to tweak a little more out of the pickups in terms of signal size and quality.

When the pickups are too far from the strings the signal will be weak and not enough to drive the amplifier. In addition to this they will tend to produce a lot of buzz which will lower the quality of the sound that is produced by them. However, having the pickups too close to the strings will cause the magnetic field to interfere with the string vibrations causing horrible pitch distortions which will sound really bad. It is the vintage pickups which suffer the most from being poorly setup. The more modern lace sensor pickups are less prone to problems due to their design and can be set a lot closer to the strings.

In order to set up the pickup heights you will need some way of measuring the distance between the string and the pickup. The best things to use are some feeler gauges like the ones used to set spark plug gaps in car engines. If you haven't got these then you can try to do it using a steel rule.

Make sure that you have finished setting up the action of your guitar and the truss rod before setting the pickup heights. Start with the bridge pickup. Fret the strings on the last fret at the body end of the guitar.

Fretting at last fret to check height of bass end of pickups

Use a Philips screw driver to turn the screws of the bridge pickup so that the distance between the strings and the pickup on both the sides of the pickup is somewhere between 3.0 mm and 2.5 mm.

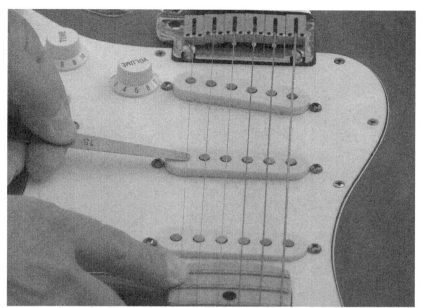

Checking the middle pickup height with feeler gauges

Once you have done this you should play some chords at different positions up and down the neck. Listen very carefully for the balance between the thick bass strings and the thin high strings. If you find that the bass strings sound too loud then you should turn the screw to lower the pickup slightly on that side. Do this, until you get the sound balance the way that you want it. In a similar fashion if you find that the high strings sound too loud in the balance then you need to lower the pickup on that side.

49

Adjusting treble side of bridge pickup

Adjusting bass side of bridge pickup

50

Move on to the middle pickup and once again fret the strings at the last fret nearest to the body. Adjust the pickup heights so that they too are also between 2.5 mm and 3.0 mm from the strings on both the bass and treble side of the pickup. As before compare the balance between the bass string side and treble string sides of the pickup. Play some chords and adjust the pick up so that you get the right balance. The next stage is to listen to the balance between the bridge and middle pickup. Raise or lower the pickup equally on each side until you get the signal output the same for each one.

Adjusting the treble side of the middle pickup

Adjusting the bass side of the middle pickup

Go onto the neck pickup and adjust this in the same way, setting it at 2.5 mm to 3.0 mm from the strings. Adjust its bass and treble balance across the pickup and then change the height of the pickup to make it roughly the same as the neck and middle pickup. Having done all of these adjustments you should have a guitar which has that classic Stratocaster sound.

Adjusting the treble side of the neck pickup

Adjusting the bass side of the neck pickup

These are the recommended settings for some different fender models. The string heights are given for the bass side of the pickup and the treble side of the pickup.

Model	Bass	Treble
Texas Special:	3.6 mm	2.4 mm
Vintage:	2.4 mm	2 mm
Noiseless:	3.2 mm	2.4 mm
Standard Single Coil:	2 mm	1.6 mm
Humbucker pickup:	1.6 mm	1.6 mm
Lace Sensor:	as close as you need them without rattling	

This doesn't mean to say that these are the settings that you will prefer. You should use your own judgement when considering the sounds that are produced.

Floating the tremolo

The Fender tremolo system has been used to great effect for many years, but it does take some setting up to make it work well. The basic idea is that you should be able to move the tremolo arm both upwards and downwards. This means that you can get both increases and decreases in the pitch of the strings. If the tremolo plate is set so that it hard against the body you will only get increases in pitch because you can only pull the tremolo bar upwards. The ideal situation is to have it set above the body. This is what is meant by the term floating.

The tremolo system can be held in this position because of the force generated by the large springs in the cavity on the back of the guitar. This is how you set up a tremolo system to float in this way.

Back of tremolo plate floating above guitar body

Use a Phillips screw driver to remove the screws in the back plate covering the tremolo springs.

Removing the tremolo back plate

One it is removed check how many springs are fitted in the body cavity. There are fixings for 5 springs. It has been found that the tremolo system floats best when only 3 springs are used.

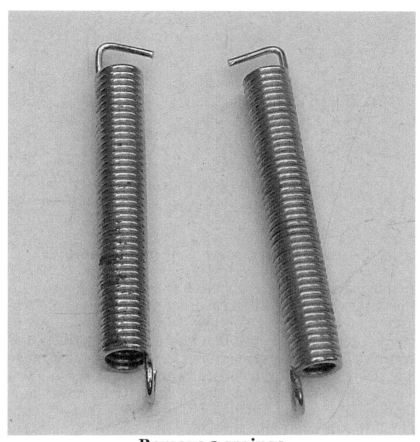

Remove 2 springs

If you find that there 5 springs used in your guitar you need to reduce it to 3. To do this remove the fourth and second spring leaving just three. The springs simply unclip from the hooks on the body claw attachment and the tail piece block. Put your springs away safely in case you decide to use them again at a later date.

3 springs in place after 2nd and 4th removed

Removing the springs will have reduced the tension on the strings and they will have drastically lowered in pitch. You therefore need to retune your guitar back up to concert pitch. Make sure that you do it a few times and play and stretch the strings a few times to try and remove any slack in the system. Once the guitar stays in tune you should check to see if the bridge of the tremolo system is floating above the body. You should find that you can move the tremolo arm up and down easily. If you find that the tremolo system is still not floating, you will need to adjust the tension on the springs in the back cavity of the guitar. The claw screws directly into the body of the guitar and has an earth wire attached to it.

Claw and adjuster screws

You need to unscrew the screws in the claw so that it moves away from the body. Only do a slight adjustment. The claw should only move a few mm. The guitar will once again have gone out of tune so you should retune it and once again check to see if the tremolo plate is floating on top of the body. Once you have got the tremolo unit to float you will need to set its floating position for optimal movement of the tremolo arm. This occurs when the gap between the back of the tremolo unit and the body of the guitar is around 3mm. Don't forget that the guitar has to be in tune for this measurement to mean anything. If the gap between the tremolo and the body is more than 3mm you need to need to tighten the screws in the claw. This will tend to force the tremolo plate back down towards the body. If the gap is less than 3 mm you will need to loosen the screws in the claw. Check after each adjustment and retune until you get the gap correctly to 3mm. When you have finished, the gap is correct and the guitar is in tune you should replace the back plate and try out your new floating tremolo system.

Truss rods

Guitar necks that are purely made out of wood will tend to bend as the strings are tuned up. This is because the string tension puts a considerable force onto the neck which causes it to bend so that the fret board appears to have a concave curve along its length. This curve can pull the strings away from the fret board giving poor playing performance and intonation problems. This is not a problem with guitars that have gut or nylon strings. This is because the tension for these strings is far lower than the metal strings used for electric guitars. One way round this problem would be to make the neck a lot thicker but this isn't what guitarists want for easier and better playing. In order to deal with this problem a rod is put in the back of the neck to apply an opposing force which will help to straighten the neck out.

On a Stratocaster the rod is under the strip of darker inlay wood seen on the back of the neck. This is called the truss rod. The top end of the truss rod emerges at the head stock end and will either be in a shallow cavity or in the form of a bullet shape projecting out of the head stock. Both types of truss rod are adjusted by the use of a hex spanner which is inserted into the end of the rod.

Guitar necks don't want to be absolutely straight because the strings need some clearance over the frets lower down the fret board when different notes are played. With the curve of the neck being convex the situation gets even worse. The ideal shape is to have a very slight concave shape to the neck profile. In this way the clearance for the frets at the bottom of the fret board is achieved. As stated before if the bow in the neck is too concave then you will be having high action problems. In general most necks are set up correctly and you might not need to adjust the truss rod ever. So long as you are happy with the way your guitar is playing then the best thing is to leave it alone. Don't mess with something that is already fixed! Times where adjustment of the truss rod may give an improvement in the playability of a guitar include: when you change the gauge of the strings drastically for example between .008 sets and .010 sets and the other way round; putting a new neck on a guitar; if the frets are very worn and you can't afford to have somebody stone down the frets.

The first thing to do is to work out if there is a problem or not. The easiest way to do this is to sight down the neck along the side edge of the fret board to see what sort of bend is actually in it. When doing this you need to make sure that you sight along he tops of the frets. If you look along the binding below the frets you will get the wrong idea because these often vary in how they are fitted along the length of the neck. It is the frets and surface of the fret board that we are interested in. If you see a slight concave bend in the fret board as you sight down the neck your guitar is probably set up correctly. If the neck has no curve in it or is bent the other way giving a convex profile then you will need to adjust the truss rod. If the profile is very curved in a concave way then once again there will be some adjustment needed to the truss rod.

Another way of checking on the curve in the neck is to use a long steel rule. Place the edge of the rule along the length of the fret board and then look at the rule sideways on. If there is no gap under the rule in the centre or it wobbles up and down as you are trying to place it along the length then the neck is either too flat or convex in shape. If there is a small gap towards the centre of the rule then the setting is probably right. If there is a large gap under the centre of the rule then the neck is probably too concave. There will of course be other indications that the neck is not set right. These could be such things as the inability to set a low action for the guitar without lots of buzzing or the inability to set the action because it is always too high.

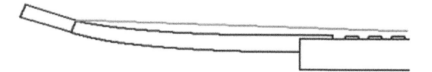

Too much string tension
Tighten Truss Rod

Truss rod too tight
Slacken off truss rod

Truss rod just right with
Slight bow in neck profile

You can next check to see if the settings match those laid down by Fender. With the guitar tuned to concert pitch put a capo on the first fret. Next fret the 6th string at the fret where the neck joins the body. Take some feeler gauges and check the gap between the string and the surface of the 8th fret. The recommended size for this gap is about 0.10 inches.

Capo 1st fret, fret at body joint and feeler gauge at 8th fret

Once you have decided that the truss rod needs adjusting then the first thing to do is to decide who is going to do it. A lot of people get scared about adjusting truss rods because there are many tales of people over tightening them a breaking the rod inside the neck. This then, would be very costly to repair. If you are scared about doing it to your favorite guitar then it is best leaving it to an expert. If you are confident about what you are doing then you shouldn't have any problem. The best thing to do first is to practice on a guitar that is relatively inexpensive before you tackle that vintage Fender Stratocaster. This is what I did. Once I had set up a few cheaper guitars and then sorted out few of my friend's guitars I was happy to have a look at my 70s Stratocaster!

The procedure for adjusting the truss rod of a guitar is pretty much the same for all guitars. If anything Stratocasters are pretty easy. Insert the correct size hex spanner into the truss rod adjuster in the head stock of the guitar. Turn it a little until it fits into the hex socket of the truss rod.

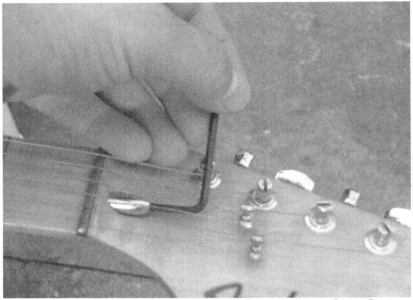

Hex spanner in bullet style truss rod end

Alternative truss rod adjuster opening

You need to decide which way you need to turn the spanner to get the correct adjustment. If the neck had a concave curve in it you need to tighten the truss rod so that it gives a force against the tension in the strings. This will then reduce the concave bow and give a flatter neck profile. In order to tighten the truss rod you need to turn the spanner in a clockwise motion in the same way as you tighten a nut on a bolt. Make only small adjustments at a time no more than half a turn. Once you have made this adjustment you need to check the gap at the 8th fret once again with the feeler gauges. Each time you do this; make sure that the guitar is still tuned to concert pitch. If the adjustment isn't enough then you need to go through the procedure again until you get the effect that you want. Be careful when tightening the truss rod because over tightening it can break the rod. This is the reason for using small adjustments and constantly checking on the result. If you find that turning the adjuster is having the opposite effect on the curvature of the neck then you are probably turning it the wrong way and as a result you should turn it the other way.

If your neck is too flat or has a convex bow then the truss rod is applying too much force to the neck. This can happen if you go from very thick gauges of strings to very thin gauges. In this case you need to slacken off the truss rod. Turn the adjuster in an anti clockwise way as if you were undoing a nut from a bolt. Once again it is very important to make small adjustments of no more than half a turn and to check the results before adjusting the rod any more. Once you have finished your adjustments make sure that the guitar is at concert pitch and remove the hex spanner from the truss rod adjuster.

The truss rod adjuster shouldn't be left loose. You should have at least a quarter of a turn on it. If you find that there is a huge amount of resistance when turning the adjuster in either direction or that there is still a convex bow in the neck even when the truss rod adjuster is completely loose you should seek advice from a professional luthier.

Guitar intonation

The intonation of your guitar is very important. This determines whether all of the parts of the guitar are in tune with each other. It is time to look at the intonation if you find that the guitar sounds out of tune when you play on different parts of the fret board or if you have just finished setting up the action of your guitar. This is especially so if the open strings always sound in tune but the fretted notes don't.

Intonation is the problem if chords played in the open position sound ok but those played at the 5th fret and higher sound out of tune. Intonation problems may also make you want to keep retuning your guitar because it keeps sounding out of tune at different positions on the fret board. In extreme cases even different open string chords can sound out of tune as well.

If you aren't sure that there is a problem then you should perform the following test. It is best to do these tests with the guitar freshly strung with new strings. Make sure that you tune the open strings with a tuner and check that they are in tune. Play an open D chord. This should also sound in tune. If it doesn't sound in tune check the open string tuning once again. When the open D is in tune move the chord shape down to the 12th fret and play it once again with the open D and A strings. This chord should ring out nicely and sound in tune as well. Do the chord move a few times making sure that the open chord tuning hasn't shifted at all. If the 2 chords sound in tune then it is likely that your intonation is correct. If the chord at the 12th fret sounds out of tune, it is a sure thing that you have intonation problems. This technique checks out the higher strings. To check further across the neck try moving the open A and open E chords down to the 12th fret. The more out of tune that these chords sound the greater the intonation problems that you have with your guitar.

To check more specifically for the intonation on individual strings you should employ the following method using an electronic tuner. Take the strings one at a time. It doesn't really matter where you start but it is probably best to start at one end and work across so that you can see any trends that may occur. Use the electronic tuner to tune the string that you want to check. You must make sure that this is done accurately and that the tuning doesn't drift. If your tuning does drift then try and solve that first by looking at the first section of this book on solving tuning problems. Once the string is in tune proceed down to the 12th fret and sound the harmonic note. You do this by resting your fretting finger lightly on the string above the 12th fret but not actually fretting the string. Pluck the string and quickly release your 12th fret finger. This should sound the harmonic note which has a ringing kind of quality to it.

Sounding the harmonic not at the 12th fret for the bass E string

Check the tuning of the harmonic. It should be the same as the open string note. If it isn't then your tuning has drifted and you need to do it again. Once the harmonic note is seen to be in tune you should fret the note at the 12th fret. Make sure that you press straight down on the string. Don't bend the string up or down or press to hard. Just lightly fret the string as carefully as you can. Once the note is accurately fretted pluck the string and then check on what note is produced on the tuner.

Playing and plucking the note fretted at the 12th fret on the bass E string

For the intonation to be correct, on this string, the note should be exactly the same as the harmonic note. Check this a few times by sounding the harmonic and fretted note each time. This will remove any doubt caused by miss fretting or bending the string. If it is flat or sharp by any amount you will have to adjust the intonation.

Check the other strings in the same way by getting them to produce harmonic notes at the 12th fret and comparing the tuning with the actual note sounded when fretting at the 12th fret. If the notes are the same for a particular string then you don't need to do anything about it, as the intonation is correct. Make a note of those strings where the intonation is not correct and then use the following method to correct the intonation problems on each string. The technique is quite simple but can take a while to do. Fortunately once the intonation is set you shouldn't have to do anything else about it unless you adjust the action, change to a different gauge of string or set the truss rod.

Intonation problems are caused by the fact that as you press down the string to fret it the string becomes slightly stretched. It is this stretching that changes the fretted note compared to the harmonic note sounded at the 12th fret. In order to compensate for this stretching you have to make the string a little longer. To do this adjust the Phillips screw in the back of the bridge saddle. You will need the correct size screwdriver to do this.

Adjusting intonation of the bass E string

Set up the harmonic check again at the 12th fret of the string that you want to adjust. Insert the screwdriver in the screw and turn it. If the note shown on the tuner is sharp compared to the harmonic note you should make the string longer by screwing in the screw. This means turning it clockwise. If the string was flat on the tuner compared to the harmonic note you need to shorten the string. Do this by turning the screw anticlockwise or screwing it out. Make your adjustments in small amounts and then check the result by retuning the string and comparing the fretted note and harmonic note at the 12th fret. If after you have done this a few times you find that the tuning is going further away from the correct note it may mean that you have been turning it the wrong way, so repeat the adjustments but in the opposite direction. You must make sure that you tune the open string after each adjustment before checking with the tuner.

Repeat the adjustments for the other strings that were found to be out. When you play the guitar after making all of the intonation adjustments you should find that chords will sound in tune no matter where you play them on the neck and that they will have a real fresh ringing tone to them. It is important that you do checks and adjustments of intonation on fresh new strings. This is because wear and dirt accumulation on old strings can make them stop vibrating in a predictable regular way along their length. This would mean that any adjustments that you make would be wrong once you put new strings on your guitar.

Keeping guitar strings clean

Keeping your guitar strings clean is very important as is changing them on a regular basis. Dirty and corroded strings can easily give the impression that there is something wrong with your guitar. Dirty strings sound dull and often lack volume. This may make you think that there is something wrong with the pickup settings or the electronics in the tone and volume circuitry. In addition to this worn and dirty strings don't vibrate in the same regular way that new strings do. This can then make you think that there are problems with the intonation of the guitar. As a result before you start making drastic adjustments to your Stratocaster think about whether it is simply the strings that are the problem. You could save yourself a lot of time and effort by doing this first.

You can make your strings last longer by keeping them in good condition. Dirt and sweat are the cause of the problem. These get trapped in the windings and the acidic nature of sweat means that you have the ideal conditions for metal corrosion to take place. To stop this happening you should keep your strings clean. Clean them after every time that you play the guitar. Use a none fluffy piece of cotton cloth, a clean handkerchief is ideal. Keep this in your guitar case so that it is always ready and waiting for you to use when you put your guitar away. Wrap the cloth round each string and rub it up and down the strings a few times. Make sure that you are actually cleaning the underneath of the string and not just the top. You should see the dirt forming tram lines as you go from one string to the next. Once the strings are clean put it back into its case and make sure that you have some bags of silica gel to absorb any extra moisture in the atmosphere of the case because this can cause corrosion as well. Even when the guitar is left in the case you should make sure that you wipe over the strings every now and then. You should also store your guitar in a dry place free from damp.

Dealing with noisy electronic components

You may have noticed that the volume and tone controls on your Stratocaster have become noisy when you turn them. This can result in a whole host of undesirable crackles and bangs as you play. You may find that the signal even cuts out altogether. This obviously isn't very helpful when you are trying to play your best guitar solo. Fortunately there is a way to return these controls to near perfect condition saving the expense of buying replacement components.

You need to buy a spray contact cleaner for electrical items. You can get this easily enough through EBay. The cleaner will help to remove the dirt and debris from the controls so that they allow electrical signals to pass more easily through them. Don't be tempted to use WD40 instead of the contact cleaner. The reason for this is that some of the ingredients in WD40 can damage the important electrical contact surfaces within the controls.

Switch cleaner with extension pipe top spray in controls

In order to clean them you have to gain access to the back of tone and volume controls under the Stratocaster scratch plate. You have to be able to remove the scratch plate from the body of the guitar.

Loosening the screws on the scratch plate

You therefore need to be in a situation where the strings are removed completely from the guitar. A good time to do this is therefore when you decide to change the guitar strings and clean off the fret board as well. You can then get a lot of these jobs done at the same time. If you don't want to do this, you can remove the scratch plate by first loosening the strings, removing the screws on the scratch plate and then sliding it out under the strings. You have to be careful with this method as you can easily scratch the body finish.

After the strings have been taken off or loosened you need to use a Phillips screwdriver to remove the screws fixing the scratch plate to the body. The scratch plate will then just have a single earth wire keeping it in place. You should, however, be able to lift and twist the scratch plate to expose the wiring underneath. If you look carefully at the back of the controls you should see that there is a hole in the side of each. This hole is only quite small so you need to attach the thin tube that came with the contact cleaner to its nozzle. Once you have done this poke the end of the tube into the hole in the side of a control and give it a short burst of the spray. If you spray too much the excess will just run out and go onto the scratch plate. Make sure that the liquid contact cleaner doesn't get onto the finish of the guitar as it may affect it in some cases. You can use a cloth or paper towels to keep the scratch plate isolated from the body of the guitar.

Spray contact cleaner into the holes in the back of the controls

After spraying the control make sure that you turn it a few times from maximum to minimum. This will distribute the cleaner over the control surface cleaning them up. Repeat the procedure on the other controls on the scratch plate. You can also spray the switch contacts as well because these can also get noisy with time. In this case move the switch several times through all of the positions to spread the cleaner over the switch contacts. You can try plugging the guitar into an amp and then turning the controls to check that the noise has stopped. If it hasn't fixed it you can repeat the cleaning procedure. Dry up any excess cleaner on the scratch plate and then fix it back onto the body with the screws.

The jack socket on the body of the guitar can also become noisy as well, due to corrosion and dirt on its surfaces. The easiest way to deal with this is to spray some of the cleaner onto the metal end of one of the jack plugs on your guitar lead. Poke this into the guitar jack socket in order to spread the cleaner onto the contact surfaces. If the problem is really bad you can even spray a short blast of the cleaner into the hole of the jack socket. Once again put the jack lead into the socket a few times to work the cleaner onto the jack contact surfaces.

Cleaning the Guitar

You will have cleaned certain parts of the guitar hardware as you have followed through this setup manual. There are plenty of other hardware parts that could also benefit from a clean every now and then. Sweat can build up on metal parts such as the bridge and machine heads and this can corrode away the surfaces making them look worn and old. Dirt and dust can get into electronic components stopping then working as well as they can.

Once you have set up your Stratocaster and it is playing like a dream you can turn your attention to the body of the guitar. Although cleaning the guitar body won't necessarily improve the playability of the guitar it can give you a feel good factor that will improve your playing.

Cleaning the Stratocaster will help to protect all of the surfaces on your guitar. The best time to clean the whole of your guitar is when you have had to take all of the strings off the instrument. You will need to get some guitar polish and a fret board lubricant and cleaner. Polishing cloths and an old tooth brush will also be used. If you haven't got guitar polish then you should find that ordinary household furniture polish will do just as good a job. These days household polish is designed to work on a number of different surfaces.

Take the fret board lubricant and cleaner and spray it onto the fret board. Use the cloth to work it into the surface of the fret board. Dirt and sweat tends to build up right next to the frets so you may need to use the tooth brush in order to remove it. Once all the sweat and dirt has been removed from the fret board, use a polishing cloth to clean off any of the polish that has been left in excess on the fret board.

For the body and metal hardware spray each with the guitar polish. Work the polish into all the nooks and crannies around the metal hardware and controls. Make sure that the back of the neck has been well cleaned and polished so that all sticky residues have been removed. Buff up the surfaces with a clean cloth to produce a lovely shine on the body of the guitar.

Conclusion

Once you have set up your Stratocaster you shouldn't have to do much to it for some time, unless you change the gauge of your strings. This is the reason that it is best to check out everything at the same time. Get it right and then forget about it and then you can get on with doing what you do best....Playing!

Not only will you be able to set up a Stratocaster you should now have the skills and experience to go on a set up other styles of guitar. If anything, these should be less complicated than a Strat. You will also save money through not having to pay out for a luthier to do basic set ups on your instruments. As well as this you will have set up your Stratocaster exactly the way that you want it. If you give the job to somebody else they will always set it up the way that they are used to or the way that they like it. Setting your Stratocaster up yourself will give you truly customized guitar.

About the Author

Jan Nasser has played many different guitars over the years but quickly fell inlove with the Fender Stratocatser design. His favourite one is a 1977 natural finish with black pickups and scratch plate. Although the 1970 large headstock versions have had some bad press over the years it has lately been reconised that the design has certain merits. The more curved finger board has a more pleasing feel to it together with the slimmer designed neck. It is unfortunate that some of them didn't quite get made as well as others. However, the key to success with these guitars is to get a good one!

As with all guitars Stratocasters can benefit greatly from a good setup. Jan quickly realized the benefits of being able to tweak a guitar to your own personal needs. This happened after paying people to set up guitars only to find that they just didn't suit his own personal playing. There is nothing better than having a set up customized to your own needs and abilities.

Even small changes to the setup of a Stratocaster can make considerable differences to the way that it plays and sounds. As a result you should take your time and change things slowly and test and test again until you are sure that the guitar is exactly how you want it. This is more of an evolutionary process, rather than a set and forget technique.

If you take your time, and think about what you are doing and why, you should find that your guitar will fit like a glove as well as producing the sounds that you always dreamt of.

Made in the USA
Middletown, DE
10 July 2020